TOUGH TERMINATORS

Twelve of the Earth's Most Fascinating Predators

By Sneed B. Collard III

NorthWord
PRESS, INC

Minocqua, Wisconsin

For Larry Pringle.
Everlasting thanks for your
guidance, humor, and
quest for a better world.

Edited by Greg Linder
Designed by Patricia Bickner Linder

Published by: NorthWord Press, Inc.
               P.O. Box 1360
               Minocqua, WI 54548

For a free catalog describing NorthWord's line of nature books and gifts, call 1-800-336-5666.

Library of Congress Cataloging-in-Publication Data

Collard, Sneed B.
        Tough Terminators / by Sneed Collard.
            p.   cm.
        Includes bibliographical references.
        Summary: Provides information about such predatory animals and plants as tigers,
    octopuses, ladybugs, and pitcher plants.
        ISBN 1-55971-223-6 : $9.95
        1. Predation (Biology)—Juvenile literature. 2. Predatory animals—Juvenile literature.
    3. Carnivorous plants—Juvenile literature. [1. Predatory animals. 2. Animals—Food habits.
    3. Carnivorous plants.]   I. Title.
    QL758.C67   1994
    574.5'3—dc20   93–19627
                                                          CIP
                                                          AC

Printed in Singapore

TABLE OF CONTENTS

About Predators

In some science fiction movies, a "terminator" is an awful, computer-controlled robot whose only purpose is to hunt and kill people. Fortunately, there's no such thing as a robot terminator in real life. However, there is a group of living things that survives by hunting and eating animals. They're called **predators**, and they are some of the most amazing creatures on Earth.

At first, it might seem disgusting to think that some animals catch and eat other animals, but there are good reasons why predators live this way. If all life forms ate only plants, there wouldn't be nearly enough food to go around. Meat also provides important nutrients and protein that can be difficult to get from plants. Predation is such a successful way to live that it has evolved in almost every group of animals. As you'll see later in the book, even some *plants* are predators.

Predators are essential to life on Earth. They help control the numbers of wild animals, so populations don't overrun their environments. Predators keep wildlife populations healthy by hunting animals that are sick or weak. By eating pests, predators prevent the spread of diseases and reduce damage to crops. All in all, predators help our environment stay balanced and healthy.

People don't always appreciate predators as much as they should. In fact, humans have done their best to hunt and exterminate most of Earth's big predators. Why? For many reasons. One reason is that people are afraid of some predators. A second reason is that predators often compete with people for food by hunting the same animals. But mostly, people have killed predators because they haven't understood the animals very well. Most of the killing isn't necessary. People and predators can almost always live together peacefully.

The following pages contain some of the world's most exciting predators. Prepare to meet 12 "tough terminators" face to face— and to find out how they make our world a better place.

Tiger

FAST FACTS

▶ **Scientific Name . . .**
Neofelis tigris
(NEE-OH-FEE-LIS TIE-GRIS)
▶ **Kind of Animal . . .**
Mammal
▶ **Order of Mammals . . .**
Carnivores
▶ **Family of Carnivores . . .**
Felids or "Cats"
▶ **Greatest Weight . . .**
662 pounds
▶ **Greatest Length . . .**
11 feet (from head to tail)
▶ **Lifespan . . .**
12 to 20 years

Tigers are the world's largest cats. Their sharp teeth are built for stabbing and cutting, while their claws whip in and out like flashing razors. Tigers and other cats belong to the group of mammals called **carnivores**. Carnivores are animals that eat meat.

A tiger usually hunts alone. It can't run very far, so it has to surprise other animals in order to catch them. The tiger sneaks up silently on its prey, then pounces.

Tigers often hunt at night. In the back of their eyes is a mirror-like layer called the **tapetum** (TUH-PEET-UM) that helps tigers—and other nocturnal animals—see in the dark.

Like most cats, tigers are highly intelligent. One tiger in India learned a special hunting method. Some of the nearby deer ate plants in the middle of a pond, where the tiger couldn't surprise them. To catch the deer, the tiger learned to race out of the trees and jump straight into the water. Then other tigers learned the trick from the first tiger.

■ Today

▨ 100 years ago

A hundred years ago, tigers lived from Iran to China and from Siberia to Indonesia. Today, most tigers live in India and southeast Asia.

To survive, wild tigers need to eat an animal the size of a full-grown deer every two weeks or so. Tigers have been known to attack young elephants and rhinoceroses, but mostly they feed on deer, wild pigs, and smaller animals. To make sure they get enough food, they stake out hunting grounds, or territories. One territory can cover hundreds of square miles.

Tigers are among the few predators that are dangerous to people. During the 1920s, tigers killed about 1,000 people per year in India. Today, tigers kill dozens of people each year in Bangladesh and southeast India. But most tigers avoid humans. Tiger attacks usually happen in places where people have invaded the tiger's territory.

Like most wild cats, the tiger has been relentlessly hunted by people. Expanding human populations have also left few wild places where the tiger can live. To help save the tiger in India, conservation groups and the Indian government started Project Tiger. The project created 19 parks where tigers can live safely and taught the Indian people how to get along with their predator neighbors. Project Tiger has helped India's tiger population double—from 2,000 to about 4,000 animals.

Ladybird Beetle

▶ **Kind of Animal . . .**
Insect
▶ **Order of Insects . . .**
Beetles
▶ **Family of Beetles . . .**
Coccinellids or "Ladybird" beetles
▶ **Weight . . .**
Less than 1/100th of an ounce
▶ **Length . . .**
Between .03 and .71 inches
▶ **Lifespan . . .**
One to three years

Predators don't have to be big like the tiger. They don't have to live in wild jungles or forests, either. One of the world's hungriest predators is a small animal you can find in your back yard—the ladybird beetle, or ladybug.

MARY CLAY/TOM STACK AND ASSOCIATES

The habitats where ladybird beetles live all have one thing in common: food. A few kinds of ladybugs eat leaves and fungus, but most are predators. They catch aphids, mites, and tiny insects called scales.

Like other insects, ladybird beetles live their lives in two major stages. After they hatch from eggs, they are called **larvae** (LAR-VEE). Ladybird beetle larvae look a little like caterpillars. They can't fly like adult beetles can, but they have healthy appetites. A hungry larva can devour 300 aphids in a single day.

As it grows, a larva moults or "sheds its skin" four or fiv times. After several weeks, it forms a cocoon. Inside this safe refuge, the larva grows into an adult. Like larvae, adul ladybird beetles eat hundreds of aphids and other insects every day.

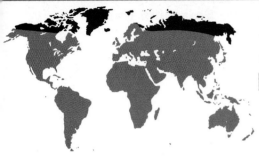

There are over 4,500 species of ladybird beetles. They live all over the world and in many different kinds of places, or habitats.

Where ladybird beetles live

Many predators have powerful eyes and ears to help them find their prey, but not ladybird beetles. Both larvae and adult beetles find other animals by "bumping into" them. Larvae can starve to death if they don't bump into something within a day or two after they hatch. If adults don't find food, they fly to a new plant or a new place and search for food there.

LADYBIRD PEST CONTROL

Farmers love ladybird beetles. In the 1890s, Australian ladybird beetles were imported to California so they could eat a kind of scale that was destroying orange trees. The ladybird beetles ate so many that they saved California's citrus industry. Using ladybird beetles and other predators to eat pests helps farmers avoid using dangerous pesticides to protect their crops.

North Pacific Giant Octopus

FAST FACTS

▶ **Scientific Name . . .**
Enteroctopus dofleini
ENTER-OK-TOH-PUSS DO-FLEEN-EYE
▶ **Kind of Animal . . .**
Cephalopod, or
"Head-footed mollusk"
▶ **Order and Family of Cephalopods . . .**
Octopods or "eight-footeds"
▶ **Greatest Weight . . .**
600 pounds
▶ **Greatest Armspan . . .**
31 feet
▶ **Lifespan . . .**
Three to five years

Like ladybird beetles, octopuses are **invertebrates**—animals without backbones. There are about 200 species of octopuses, but the North Pacific giant octopus is one of the largest.

DAVE B. FLEETHAM/TOM STACK AND ASSOCIATES

Octopuses are shy, but they're smart. They have the largest brains and are the most intelligent of all invertebrates. In experiments, octopuses have learned how to unscrew the lids of jars so they can reach the food inside.

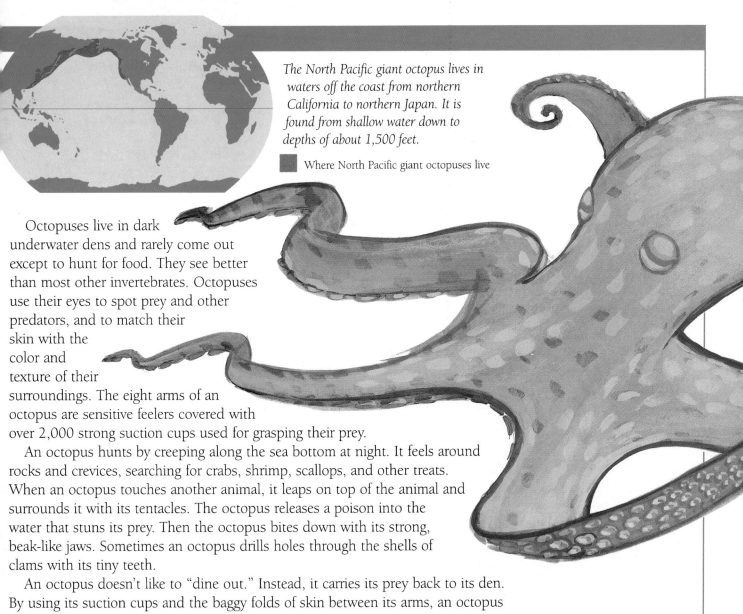

The North Pacific giant octopus lives in waters off the coast from northern California to northern Japan. It is found from shallow water down to depths of about 1,500 feet.

■ Where North Pacific giant octopuses live

Octopuses live in dark underwater dens and rarely come out except to hunt for food. They see better than most other invertebrates. Octopuses use their eyes to spot prey and other predators, and to match their skin with the color and texture of their surroundings. The eight arms of an octopus are sensitive feelers covered with over 2,000 strong suction cups used for grasping their prey.

An octopus hunts by creeping along the sea bottom at night. It feels around rocks and crevices, searching for crabs, shrimp, scallops, and other treats. When an octopus touches another animal, it leaps on top of the animal and surrounds it with its tentacles. The octopus releases a poison into the water that stuns its prey. Then the octopus bites down with its strong, beak-like jaws. Sometimes an octopus drills holes through the shells of clams with its tiny teeth.

An octopus doesn't like to "dine out." Instead, it carries its prey back to its den. By using its suction cups and the baggy folds of skin between its arms, an octopus can carry up to a dozen crabs at a time.

Many stories have been told about giant octopuses attacking people, but most of these stories are not true. Once in a while a giant octopus will leap onto a scuba diver, but the octopus rarely bites. The animal is usually just curious, and it soon lets go. Most scuba divers feel lucky to be "attacked" by one of the ocean's most intelligent and beautiful predators.

Aplomado Falcon

FAST FACTS

▶ **Scientific Name . . .**
Falco femoralis
(FAL-KOH FEEM-OR-AL-ISS)
▶ **Kind of Animal . . .**
Bird
▶ **Order of Birds . . .**
Falconiformes or
"Birds of Prey"
▶ **Greatest Weight . . .**
One pound
▶ **Greatest Wingspan . . .**
35 inches
▶ **Lifespan . . .**
12 to 20 years

A falcon kills its prey with a flash of silver feathers and a *whack*. Peregrine falcons are famous for their speed—up to 217 miles per hour in a full dive. But another "top gun" that often gets overlooked is the aplomado (AH-PLO-MAH-DOE) falcon.

KENNETH W. FINK/PHOTO RESEARCHERS

The aplomado falcon is a **raptor**, or bird of prey. Raptors include eagles, hawks, ospreys, kites, and falcons. Raptors are the premier hunters of the bird world.

Aplomado is a Spanish word that means "steel gray"— the color of the aplomado's back. Aplomados are not big as raptors go, but their hunting skills are breathtaking.

Like other falcons, aplomados usually hunt birds. An aplomado sits on a tree or a yucca plant, waiting patiently for another bird to come along. When a bird flies nearby, the falcon streaks after it—through trees and brush and across open plains. When it catches up, the falcon slams into the other bird with so much force that the bird's neck may be broken.

Aplomados once lived from the American Southwest all the way to Central America. Now they mostly live in the Mexican states of Veracruz, Tabasco, and Chiapas. A small population exists in Chihuahua and Coahuila.

■ Where aplomado falcons live

Male and female aplomados sometimes hunt together. If they find a bird sitting in a bush or a tree, the male tries to flush out the bird so the female can zoom in for the kill. When aplomados can't find birds to eat, they snatch rodents, lizards, and insects.

Aplomados once lived in Texas, Arizona, and New Mexico. But by 1942, they no longer nested in the U.S. Why? Because most of the open grasslands where falcons like to live had been converted to farms or were overgrown with brush. Pesticides such as DDT weakened the shells of the aplomado's eggs, so they broke before the baby birds could hatch and grow.

Since 1985, a group called The Peregrine Fund has been trying to bring the aplomado back to the Southwest by releasing young falcons. Progress has been slow, but a few aplomados now live in Texas. One day, we may all have the chance to see the brilliant silver flash of one of the Earth's most spectacular raptors.

TERRENCE MOORE

13

Saltwater Crocodile

Crocodiles are the closest living relatives to dinosaurs. There are over 20 species of crocodiles, and they are skilled hunters. Most do not bother people. One species that people *should* be careful of is the saltwater crocodile, or "saltie."

JOE McDONALD/TOM STACK AND ASSOCIATES

FAST FACTS

▶ **Species Name . . .**
Crocodylus porosus
(KROK-OH-DILL-US POR-OH-SIS)
▶ **Kind of Animal . . .**
Reptile
▶ **Order and Family of Reptiles . . .**
Crocodiles
▶ **Greatest Weight . . .**
Over 6,000 pounds
▶ **Greatest Length . . .**
30 feet
▶ **Lifespan . . .**
About 65 years

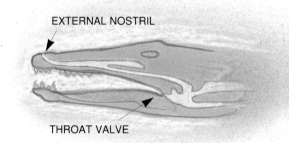

EXTERNAL NOSTRIL

THROAT VALVE

Crocodiles are especially suited to a watery lifestyle. Special valves in their throats keep water from pouring into their lungs when they swallow food or float on the water's surface. They are also excellent swimmers, pushing themselves along with their powerful tails.

Crocodile eyes—like cat eyes—capture extra light for nighttime hunting. Their sensitive ears tell them when even a tiny animal jumps into the water.

Salties eat almost everything. Underwater, they use their spike teeth to catch fish, sharks, turtles, and crabs. Near the shore, they catch monkeys, deer, boars, kangaroos, and even water buffaloes.

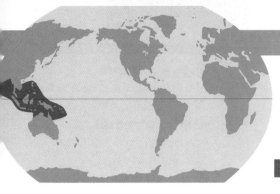

Salties live from southern India to Far East Asia and all the way to Australia. They hang out in swamps, along coasts, or in rivers. However, they sometimes travel hundreds of miles across the open ocean.

■ Where saltwater crocodiles live

Like tigers, salties surprise their prey. Crocodiles drift along, hiding in tall grass or reeds. Sometimes they dive underwater to sneak up on other animals. When they're near the prey animal, they burst out of the water with their teeth flashing. On land, crocodiles can sprint up to 30 miles per hour. They seize their victims in their jaws and swallow small animals in one gulp. Salties drag larger prey animals into deep water to drown them. Then they tear the animals into bite-sized pieces.

The saltwater crocodile is one of the largest and most dangerous of all reptiles. Salties kill several people each year in India, Australia, and New Guinea. In 1975 in Indonesia, crocodiles ate more than 40 people who spilled out of one overturned boat.

DAVE B. FLEETHAM/TOM STACK AND ASSOCIATES

Crocodiles have more to fear from people than we do from them. Salties—and most other crocodiles—have been hunted for their skins. People have made suitcases, handbags, shoes, belts, and even watch straps from the skins. In India and Asia, wild saltwater crocodiles are almost extinct. Salties have a brighter future in New Guinea and Australia, where they are protected by laws and live farther away from people.

15

Community Spider

FAST FACTS

▶ **Species Name . . .**
Stegodyphus mimosarum
(STAY-GO-DIE-FUS MIM-OH-SAIR-UM)

▶ **Kind of Animal . . .**
Arachnid (Spiders, Mites
and Scorpions)

▶ **Order of Arachnids . . .**
Spiders

▶ **Family of Spiders . . .**
Eresids

▶ **Greatest Weight . . .**
1/20 of an ounce

▶ **Greatest Length . . .**
4/10 of an inch

▶ **Lifespan . . .**
One year

Without spiders, our planet would soon be overrun by insects and other pests. There may be as many as 180,000 kinds of spiders, and all spiders are carnivorous. A spider usually hunts alone, but about half a dozen species live and hunt together. These are called **social spiders**. One social spider that scientists have studied is the community spider, or *Stegodyphus* (STAY-GO-DIE-FUS).

EDWARD S. ROSS

In Africa, the pea-sized *Stegodyphus* live in shrubs and trees on the open plains. Up to 1,000 *Stegodyphus* spiders may live together. They build huge nests that are made up of **retreats** and webs. Retreats are masses of silk where spiders find shelter. The webs are built to catch the spiders' insect prey. Webs are tough, and they can cover up to four square yards—about the area of a badminton net. By working together to build big webs, the community spiders trap more—and bigger—insects than they could if each one lived alone.

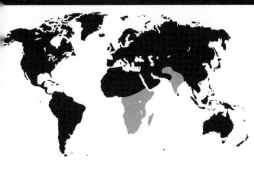

Social spiders are found in South America, Asia, and Australia. Stegodyphus *lives in southern and eastern Africa, Madagascar, and Asia.*

Where community spiders live

Stegodyphus webs trap everything from gnats and ants to wasps and praying mantises. When an insect is caught, it struggles, sending vibrations through the web. If the vibrations are small, only one or two spiders come to investigate. But if the prey is large and thrashing around, dozens of spiders rush out of the retreats.

The spiders kill a trapped insect by biting it and injecting poison into it. Then they begin to feed. Each night the community spiders repair their web in spots where it has been damaged by insects, wind, or rain.

Each *Stegodyphus* spider lives for only about a year, but *Stegodyphus* colonies can last for many years. The colonies benefit over 25 animals besides the community spiders. Several different spider species live with the *Stegodyphus* and steal their food. Wasps and moths lay their eggs on the *Stegodyphus* or in its nests. By working together, community spiders help each other survive, but they also give life to many other animals.

Great Barracuda

FAST FACTS

▶ **Species Name . . .**
Sphyraena barracuda
(SFY-REE-NA BEAR-A-COO-DA)
▶ **Kind of Animal . . .**
Fish
▶ **Order of Fishes . . .**
Perciformes or
"Perch-shaped fish"
▶ **Family of Perciformes . . .**
Sphyraenids or "Barracudas"
▶ **Greatest Weight . . .**
106 pounds
▶ **Greatest Length . . .**
6 feet
▶ **Lifespan . . .**
15 years

The sea—like the land—is a good place to live if you're a predator. You've already seen that octopuses find plenty of slow-moving prey in the ocean. But what about all those speedy ocean fish? Most predators are too slow to catch them, but not the great barracuda.

Barracudas hunt during the day. Like some sharks, they make their living by catching other fish. Young barracudas live in grassbeds and eat small fish like gobies and sardines.

By the time they are one or two feet long, barracudas stake out territories in shallow water. During most of the day, each barracuda hunts alone within its territory, which might cover several hundred square feet. When the tide comes in, though, medium-sized barracudas band together. Working as a team, they attack incoming schools of fish. When they grow larger, barracudas stop working together. Large barracudas are loners, patrolling deeper waters for puffers, needlefish, and other "fish dinners."

MIKE BACON/TOM STACK AND ASSOCIATES

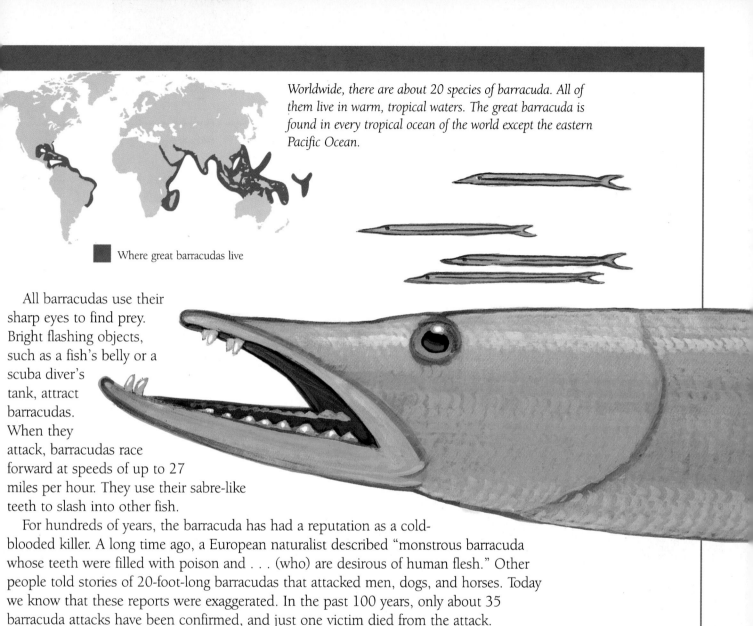

Worldwide, there are about 20 species of barracuda. All of them live in warm, tropical waters. The great barracuda is found in every tropical ocean of the world except the eastern Pacific Ocean.

Where great barracudas live

All barracudas use their sharp eyes to find prey. Bright flashing objects, such as a fish's belly or a scuba diver's tank, attract barracudas. When they attack, barracudas race forward at speeds of up to 27 miles per hour. They use their sabre-like teeth to slash into other fish.

For hundreds of years, the barracuda has had a reputation as a cold-blooded killer. A long time ago, a European naturalist described "monstrous barracuda whose teeth were filled with poison and . . . (who) are desirous of human flesh." Other people told stories of 20-foot-long barracudas that attacked men, dogs, and horses. Today we know that these reports were exaggerated. In the past 100 years, only about 35 barracuda attacks have been confirmed, and just one victim died from the attack.

By the way, eating barracudas can be dangerous. The meat from barracudas and many other tropical fish can contain a poison called **ciguatera** (SIG-WA-TAIR-UH) toxin. There is no way to know which fish are poisonous and which are not. This is too bad for seafood lovers who would like to eat a barracuda steak, but it's extra protection for the barracuda.

19

Pitcher Plant

FAST FACTS

▶ **Kind of Plant . . .**
Flowering plant
▶ **Order and Family of Flowering Plants . . .**
New World Pitcher Plants
▶ **Greatest Height . . .**
Four feet
▶ **Lifespan . . .**
10 to 30 years

By now you're probably getting the idea that being a predator is a successful way to live. If they could talk, some plants would agree. These plants are called **insectivorous** plants, because they trap and eat insects and other small animals. One especially clever insectivore is the pitcher plant.

Pitcher plants live in bogs, swamps, and other wet places where the soil is too poor for other plants. But pitcher plants *thrive* here. Why? Because other plants need to obtain nutrients from the soil, but the pitcher plant "steals" nitrogen and other nutrients from the insects it catches. And there are plenty of insects in wet places.

Pitcher plants catch insects in wonderful ways. Their leaves are shaped into modified traps called pitchers. Sweet-smelling nectar glands serve as bait for the unsuspecting prey.

KERRY T. GIVENS/TOM STACK AND ASSOCIATES

Where New World pitcher plants live

New World pitcher plants live in North and South America. We are lucky to have about ten species of pitcher plants in the United States and Canada. Most live in the southeastern U.S.

The nectar glands are concentrated near the mouth of the pitcher. Flies, moths, mosquitoes, and ants can't resist this sweet meal. When the insects get to the top of the plant, watch out! The rim and the inside surface are coated with a slippery, waxy substance. If the insect makes one false move, it's plunged into the pitcher, where it's digested in a pool of juices.

Pitcher plants are harmless to people, but they help control pests by catching hundreds of kinds of insects. Each fall, the pitchers and the flowers of the plant wither away. But the roots may live for decades, sending up fresh pitchers and flowers every spring.

Several varieties of pitcher plants are common, but others are rare and endangered. Many wet places where pitcher plants grow have been drained for building and farming. Plant collectors also dig up pitcher plants. The U.S. Fish and Wildlife Service and conservation groups are working hard to make sure that these precious plant predators survive.

21

Siphonophore

FAST FACTS

▶ **Kind of Animal . . .**
Jelly Animals
▶ **Order of Jelly Animals . . .**
Siphonophores
▶ **Greatest Weight . . .**
10 to 20 pounds
▶ **Greatest Length . . .**
Over 200 feet
▶ **Lifespan . . .**
Unknown. Perhaps hundreds
of years.

Sharks and barracudas get more attention, but siphonophores (SY-FAHN-O-FORZ) may be the most important predators in the sea. Siphonophores belong to a group of animals known as **gelatinous zooplankton**, or "jelly animals." These are soft-bodied, jellyfish-like creatures that are carried around by ocean currents.

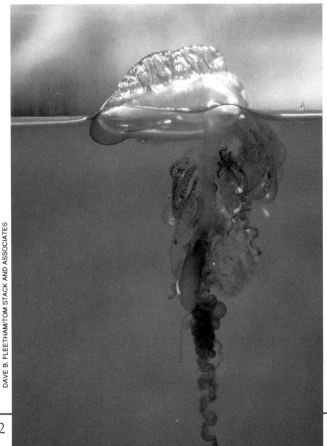

DAVE B. FLEETHAM/TOM STACK AND ASSOCIATES

People often call a siphonophore an animal, but it's really a collection or colony of little animals that work together. Some parts of the colony are good at swimming. Other parts are good at catching or digesting food. Still others specialize in reproduction.

Siphonophores hunt by using a "sit-in-waiting" strategy. A typical siphonophore stretches its body and extends dozens or even thousands of tentacles. These tentacles are often loaded with stinging cells called **nematocysts** (NEE-MAT-O-SISTS), which can stun or kill the siphonophore's prey.

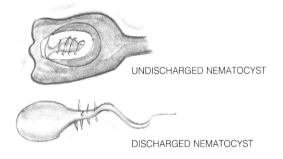

UNDISCHARGED NEMATOCYST

DISCHARGED NEMATOCYST

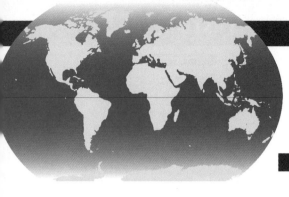

Siphonophores live in all the world's oceans. There are over 160 species, and they live from the ocean surface to depths of more than 12,000 feet.

■ Where siphonophores live

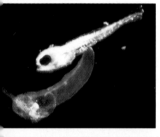

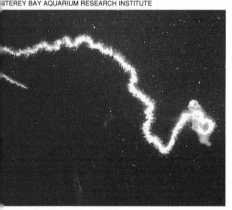

To help attract prey, some of the siphonophore's tentacles contain tiny parts that look like fish, shrimp, or jellyfish. By dangling and jiggling these "decoys," the siphonophore lures fish and other animals to their death.

Most siphonophores are small, but some reach enormous sizes. One called *Apolemia* is hundreds of feet long. It may even be the longest "animal" (or colony) in the world. When *Apolemia* hangs out its tentacles, it becomes a "wall of death" that traps thousands of animals.

Top: "Decoy" and fish larva.
Bottom: Apolemia.

The most famous kind of siphonophore is the Portugese Man-of-War, which lives in all of the world's tropical seas. The Portugese Man-of-War and several other siphonophores can deliver a powerful sting, but they're not considered deadly to people.

23

Gray Wolf

FAST FACTS

▶ **Species Name . . .**
Canis lupus
(KAY-NIS LOOP-US)
▶ **Kind of Animal . . .**
Mammal
▶ **Order of Mammals . . .**
Carnivores
▶ **Family of Carnivores . . .**
Canids or "Dogs"
▶ **Weight . . .**
33 to 176 pounds
▶ **Length . . .**
4 to 6 feet
▶ **Lifespan . . .**
8 to 20 years

No other "terminator" has inspired more fear than the wolf. In stories like "Little Red Riding Hood," wolves are villains that attack grandmothers and devour small children. But in recent times, people have discovered that wolves are not such bad guys after all.

TOM AND PAT LEESON

Wolves eat different things, depending on where they live. In desert areas, they pounce on rabbits and other small prey. Where larger prey is common, wolves hunt moose, beaver, and caribou. But wolves are fairly small, and they're not fast runners. In order to kill large animals, they often hunt in social groups called **packs**.

Each wolf pack contains between two and 20 wolves. The pack is highly organized, and it's led by two wolves—the **alpha male** and the **alpha female**. The two alpha wolves are usually the only pack members that mate, and they also lead the pack in hunting and feeding. To catch a caribou or a moose, several wolves may rush at the animal and overwhelm it. At other times, one or two wolves may trap an animal by herding it toward other wolves.

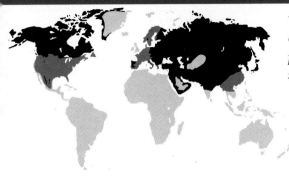

Wolves once roamed over most of the northern hemisphere—from the Arctic Circle to Mexico and even the deserts of the Middle East. Today, large wolf populations are found only in parts of Canada, Alaska, Minnesota, Iran, southeastern Europe, and the former Soviet Union.

Former wolf range

Current wolf range

Like many other predators, wolves are highly intelligent. They howl to stay in touch with each other. Younger wolves learn how and where to hunt from older wolves in the pack. As long ago as 10,000 years, people learned that they could tame and breed wolves as workers and companions. All modern dogs—from poodles to German shepherds—are descended from the tamed wolves of long ago.

There are hundreds of stories about wolves attacking and killing people. Almost all of these stories are false. Probably the biggest reason people have feared wolves is because wolves compete with us as predators. Wolves eat deer that hunters would like to shoot for themselves. Sometimes wolves feed on domestic livestock. They don't know that cows belong to a rancher or dairy farmer. To wolves, a cow simply looks like dinner.

But people and wolves can—and do—live together peacefully. Over a thousand wolves live in Minnesota, many of them near farms. In Italy, wolves live within 30 miles of Rome, a city of almost three million people. When people start to understand these predators, they realize that wolves are really shy, intelligent, and amazing animals.

TOM AND PAT LEESON

Dragonfly

FAST FACTS

▶ **Kind of Animal . . .**
Insect
▶ **Order of Insects . . .**
Odonata or "Dragonfly"
or "Darner"
▶ **Weight . . .**
Less than an ounce
▶ **Wingspan . . .**
Up to seven inches
▶ **Lifespan . . .**
Up to six years as larva,
then 40 to 50 days as adult

Dragonflies are one of the oldest groups of insects. Naturalists have found fossils of primitive dragonflies that are over 200 million years old. Some of these dragonflies had wingspans of 28 inches—the same wingspan as a small, modern-day duck or hawk.

JOHN GERLACH/TOM STACK AND ASSOCIATES

Like ladybird beetles, dragonflies are predators in both their larval and adult stages. But unlike the ladybugs, dragonflies are **opportunistic hunters**. They eat almost anything they can catch.

Dragonflies spend most of their lives as aquatic larvae, living in ponds, streams, and lakes. They moult up to 15 times, shedding their skins and growing bigger with each moult. After their final moult, they climb out of the water as adults.

Adult dragonflies may be the most spectacular fliers in the insect world. They have two pairs of wings that beat independently, allowing them to fly forward, sideways, and even backward.

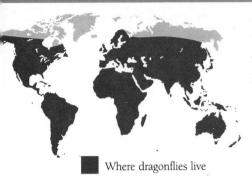

Where dragonflies live

There are over 5,000 species of dragonflies. They're most common in the tropics and near wetlands, but they live in many habitats—from deserts to high mountains to polar regions.

FLY EATING CONTEST

To help them spot their prey, dragonflies have two large eyes called "compound eyes." Each compound eye contains thousands of little eyes that give dragonflies an almost 360-degree view of their environment. Dragonflies also have three small eyes called "ocelli" on the upper parts of their heads. Ocelli do not focus on objects, but they seem to tell dragonflies how much light is around them and which way is up.

Dragonflies hunt by patrolling the air for prey or by "perching and waiting" on grasses or rocks. When a dragonfly sees something it wants to eat, it zooms forward and crashes into its prey at speeds of up to 30 miles per hour. The dragonfly captures the prey animal in a "basket" that it forms with its legs. Then it devours the animal in mid-air.

Dragonflies eat many kinds of animals that are harmful to people, including tsetse flies, horseflies, mosquitoes, aphids, and locusts. One hungry dragonfly can catch about 200 of these animals in one day.

Artists, insect collectors, and scientists have been fascinated by dragonflies for hundreds of years. But water pollution and the draining of marshes and lakes have destroyed many dragonfly homes. If these fabulous fliers are to survive for another 200 million years, we must protect our marshes, lakes, and other wetlands.

Gray Whale

FAST FACTS

▶ **Species Name . . .**
Eschrichtius robustus
(ESH-RIK-TEE-US ROW-BUST-US)

▶ **Kind of Animal . . .**
Mammal

▶ **Order of Mammals . . .**
Cetaceans or "Whales and Porpoises"

▶ **Greatest Weight . . .**
75,000 pounds

▶ **Greatest Length . . .**
49 feet

▶ **Greatest Lifespan . . .**
56 years

We don't usually think of large whales as predators. That's because big whales like the gray whale have **baleen** in their mouths instead of teeth. A whale's baleen looks like an enormous comb that fills the whale's mouth. It acts like a huge trap, and the large whales use it to catch more animals than any other kind of predator.

JAMES D. WATT/PACIFIC STOCK

Most baleen whales "filter" water through their mouths to find shrimp and other kinds of food. Gray whales feed this way, but they also eat in another way.

Unlike other whales, gray whales "graze" like deep-sea cattle along muddy sea bottoms. They dive as deep as 200 feet, then roll on their sides. When they open their mouths, they turn into the world's biggest vacuum cleaners, sucking up hundreds of pounds of mud in an instant.

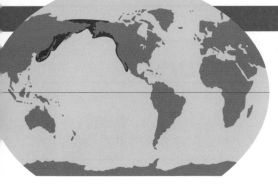

Gray whales used to live in the Atlantic and Pacific Oceans. By about the year 1700, however, Europeans had hunted Atlantic gray whales to extinction. Most gray whales now live along the western (Pacific) coast of North America.

█ Where gray whales live today

Gray whales sift through the mud for worms, crustaceans, and other invertebrates. When they've caught enough invertebrates in their baleen, the whales slurp them down with the help of their six-foot tongues. One scientist estimated that a gray whale can eat over 150,000 pounds of invertebrates in a single summer. Since most of the invertebrates weigh an ounce or less, that's a lot of sifting and grazing.

Gray whales spend their winters in Mexico, where they give birth to baby gray whales. The whales don't eat much during the winter, because food supplies are not as abundant and the whales are busy mating, giving birth, and raising their young. In spring, though, they migrate north like many birds do. In the shallow Arctic seas near Alaska, the feasting really starts. During a single summer, an adult gray whale might gain over 12,000 pounds.

Many people think that gray whales are the smartest whales of all. Whalers called them "devil fish" because their boats were often attacked by gray whales. When they're being chased, gray whales change speed, dive, and use other tricks to escape.

Whalers killed up to three-quarters of all the Pacific gray whales by the late 1800s. Fortunately, gray whales were protected by law in 1946, and today there may be more Pacific gray whales than ever. Over 20,000 grazing gray predators migrate up and down the Pacific coastline each year.

More Tough Terminators

It's not always easy to find some of the biggest predators like tigers and gray whales. But no matter where you live, predators are part of your environment. Here are a few of the "tough terminators" that might live near you:

Spiders	Foxes	Weasels
Hawks	Coyotes	Herons
Snakes	Trout	Egrets
Praying Mantises	Moles	Opossums
Frogs	Raccoons	Scorpions
Bats	Bass (the fish)	Water striders
Lizards	Bobcats	

As you may realize, predators are an important part of the world around us. They're often at the top of nature's **food webs**—a term describing the relationship that exists between plants, animals, and other organisms. Predators are at the top because they eat other animals. Without them, the balance between all the other plants and animals in the food web would be upset. For example, the overhunting of crocodiles has led to an explosion of catfish living in some rivers. With few crocodiles around to eat them, catfish have devoured all the smaller fish that people like to eat.

The removal of other predators from food webs has also led to serious consequences for the environment. That's why we must protect all plant and animal species—not just the ones that look cute or act friendly. We need to be sure that food webs are not thrown out of balance.

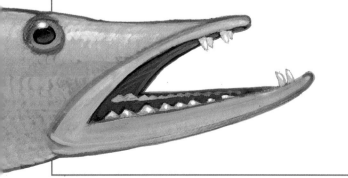

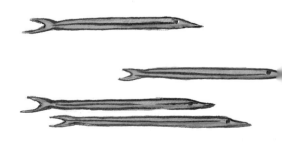

The Top Predator

By now you know a lot about predators. You've seen how predators hunt, what they eat, and where they live. But there's one group of predators we haven't talked about. They are the most important predators of all: people.

People eat many kinds of food, but for thousands of years we have eaten other animals in order to survive. Some "people predators" have hunted in forests and deserts. Other people predators have raised their own prey animals, like goats, cows, and chickens. Still others have fished the oceans and lakes for food.

Being predators has helped us survive, but our activities have also affected the earth and its creatures. Hunting has driven many species—including other predators—to extinction. By grazing on grasses, the sheep, cows, and goats we raise have turned some fertile grasslands into deserts. Overfishing has destroyed food sources in many areas. Even cats and dogs—our "pet predators"—have wiped out wildlife in some areas. On one island in New Zealand, a lighthouse keeper's cat eliminated 13 species of birds from the island.

Because we are the world's "top predators," we are the only ones who can make sure our planet remains a great place to live. We can do many things to keep our environment healthy, and one of the most important is to help other predators survive. To help small predators like ladybird beetles and dragonflies, we can keep a pond in the back yard or avoid spraying pesticides on the lawn.

To help larger predators, you can share what you've learned about them with your family and friends. You can also get more information about helping predators by writing to the groups listed on the next page. Remember that predators—whether they're people, animals, or plants—are more than tough. They're terrific!

LARRY MISHKAR

Groups That Help Predators

The Nature Conservancy
1815 North Lynne St.
Arlington, VA 22209
(Protects predators, plants, and animals
by safeguarding lands and waters)

Greenpeace Public Information
1436 U Street NW
Washington, D.C. 20009
(Works on many environmental issues,
including protection of whales and oceans)

U.S. Fish and Wildlife Service
Publications Unit
4401 North Fairfax Drive
Mail Stop 130 Webb
Arlington, VA 22203
(Works to protect endangered species,
including gray wolves and falcons)

Sierra Club
Public Affairs Department
730 Polk St.
San Francisco, CA 94109
(Works on many environmental issues, including
protection of predators and endangered species)

The Peregrine Fund Interpretive Center
5666 West Flying Hawk Lane
Boise, ID 83709
(Works to bring falcons back to their former
homes and protects other birds of prey)

Part of the price of this book is donated to groups that try to help predators.